Hang Up Your Hang Ups

By Payton Kemp Dale

Hang Up Your Hang Ups

Payton Kemp Dale

Hang Up Your Hang Ups

Dedication

This book is dedicated to every single woman who has

never felt pretty enough, thin enough, or good enough. You

are so enough that it's not even funny. This book is for you.

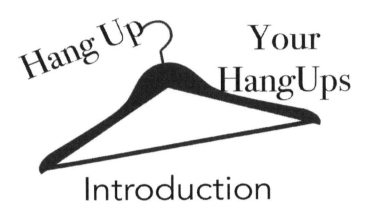

Introduction

Every single woman I know has a sob story about that one time one of their family members picked on them because of their looks. These stories are ones that haunt them forever. They cause that woman to perhaps only wear black, or to not even consider going near a pool for fear of wearing a bathing suit. I am no different. My family liked to be hyper critical of

my weight as long as I could possibly remember. The pain of disappointing the people who loved me the most lead me to unrealistic expectations of myself, which then lead me down the rabbit hole of eating disorders in my teenage years.

I knew that if I was going through this, that others must feel it too. It was then that I realized my true life's purpose was to make sure that as few people as possible felt like they were unworthy. In the long run, my pain ended up being something that I was able to channel into helping others by creating my own styling business. I have always loved clothes and accessories for the confidence they gave me, and how it felt like I was wearing a representation of who I was on the inside. Through every up and down on the scale, I learned how to dress that body to the best of my abilities. To this day, that gives me a leg up on most any other stylist around.

Hang Up Your Hang Ups

Maybe they can dress every body type, but they sure as heck hasn't been every body type!

I have worked with some of the biggest names, and some of the biggest nobodies you've never met. I have styled videos, album covers, magazine spreads, and while each project and client differ, one thing stays the same. Everyone has something they don't like about themselves.

It was in those fittings that I got really good at giving pep talks. None of it was bullshit. I believed everything I said to those men and women as they stared at their reflections. The long story short? No one cares about your flaws as much as you do. So, let's get over it and start loving ourselves.

My formula works 99.9 percent of the time. Expressing your personal style is one of the most healing forms of

self-love that I have been so fortunate to see time and time again. This isn't just another book on how many black dresses a woman needs to own. This is a book about loving yourself, and dressing like you do!

So, consider this book to be your own personal stylist giving you a pep talk. I've made it interactive, so you can answer my questions just like my regular clients would. Let's get on with it. Here is my no bullshit guide to loving yourself, and dressing like it.

Chapter One

My Back Pages

I don't ever remember not being hyper aware of my weight and my looks. From an early age, I was taught that my body was too big, too pale, and not enough to make me worthy of love, attention, and praise. This pattern continued to affect me well into adolescence.

Payton Kemp Dale

There are no photos of me from the first time I went to Disney World because I had a muffin top that day. My first ballet recital that I was really excited about wasn't documented because the too-tight leotard stretching over my large belly was too much of a distraction, and something not worthy of praise or an overpriced photo package. Swimming wasn't an option because it meant I was required to wear a bathing suit. In gym class, I often faked stomach aches to avoid wearing shorts and being teased for my jiggly thighs.

I often joke that it's a rite of passage in my family to develop your first eating disorder. Of course, it's not all that funny. It's more of a self-depreciating coping mechanism. But, it's true nonetheless.

"You have no business being that big." said my father years ago after he asked how much I weighed these days.

Hang Up Your Hang Ups

I doubt he actually remembers the conversation, but those words will stay with me forever. I weighed 172 pounds.

At the age of eighteen, standing at least a head over everyone else in my graduating class, my own father told me that there was something wrong with me. I was somehow defective because of a number on the scale. The women in my family were all petite, and my dad made it known that there was only one way to be attractive. And, as we all know in our modern society that attractive=worthy. I wasn't born big, but due to lack of appropriate nutrition and depression, I got that bloated belly pretty early in life. That bloated belly was the thing that made everyone in my family uncomfortable enough to point it out to me on a regular basis.

"I never have to worry about Payton when she goes out. I mean, the clothes she wears are practically birth control in

itself" my mother joked one night as I came down the stairs to leave for a night out with my friends. Another phrase she liked to use on a regular basis was that whatever I was wearing made me look like I was pregnant. These words cut like a knife and chipped away at my already crushed self-esteem until I had very little worth left at all. What was the point in trying to accomplish anything if all I was good for was the number on the tag of my jeans?

The programming I received early on was "You're only as good as you are thin." Thin is beautiful, and beauty is the only thing that women truly have to offer the world. The flaw in this plan was that no one really taught me how to be thin in a healthy way. My beautiful mother was half my size at the time, and she still continued to stand in front of her full-length mirror and pick herself apart from head to toe.

Hang Up Your Hang Ups

As she prodded at every single thing on herself that wasn't good enough, I looked at my own body, much larger than hers, spotted with acne scars, and decorated with tiger stripes all over, and decided that if Mom wasn't beautiful, then I would never have a shot at beauty either.

It didn't help that I was an emotional eater. The first time I ever really remembered having a blackout eating spell was right after my parents' divorced. We had just come back from staying a weekend with my dad, and my parents were at each other's throats over the phone about something or another. I snuck out of my room to the kitchen to find a box of those glorious Little Debbie cakes in the cabinets. As I retrieved one from the box, gingerly lifting the flap, and muffling the sound of the crinkling cellophane underneath my sweatshirt, I

could hear my mother in the other room, now screaming over the phone at my dad and his new wife. With each and every name called, I felt my body start to go numb. My brain went quiet. It was the first time I had shut myself down completely. Aside from blinking and breathing, my body felt like it no longer belonged to me. I greedily shoved that first cupcake into my mouth and was met with a rush of euphoria.

The numbness was gone! The sugar high hit nearly immediately, and I no longer cared about my parents hating each other, or the fact that my dad had just married a genuinely insane person. There were cupcakes! I don't remember eating the entire box that night, but I did. Almost like when an alcoholic gets blackout drunk, I blackout binged. I went to bed with a stomach ache and wondered why I would do such a thing. When I awoke the next morning with a pain

Hang Up Your Hang Ups

in my stomach, I made my way to the kitchen where Mom was making lunches for us. When she went to reach for the box of snack cakes, she looked at me with disgust in her eyes and said "Payton! Did you eat all of these cakes?! Do you KNOW how many calories are in those? They are SO FATTENING! I just bought these! How could you do that?" And from that moment on, I decided to keep my binge eating a secret. I mastered the art of keeping my binging under wraps.

I would stay up later than everyone else, sneak down to the kitchen, and do whatever I could to make that numbness go away. When I got older and could drive myself to school, I would sometimes stop at three different fast food places to get breakfast at each one. I would drink my sugary Starbucks mochas, and then get breakfast from Burger King and then McDonald's, and feel like I had a dirty little secret.

I would giggle into my McMuffin, and then walk into school covered in crumbs, and beat myself up for the rest of the day. To this day, I still fight the urge to secret eat in the car when I leave a grocery store, and in more recent years, I have killed an entire bag of chips before leaving the parking lot. Old habits die hard.

It's not exactly a surprise that I got up to nearly 200 pounds in the heyday of my binging. Instead of sitting me down and asking what was wrong with me, my parents started to take extreme measures. My stepmother at the time resorted to crushing up illegal diet pills and sneaking them into my food and drink. It wasn't until I got incredibly ill that she even acknowledged what she had done. After that fiasco, my mom suggested that I go on Weight Watchers, where calories are given points, and you are only allowed to have so

Hang Up Your Hang Ups

many of them a day.   I learned that ice cream sandwiches

were three points, and proceeded to spend an entire summer

eating my points weight in ice cream, wondering why I felt

sick all of the time. My parents allowed me to go on diet pills,

shakes, and any other "Get Thin Quick" fix they could. And,

as we all know, none of those things ever work in the long run.

Not one of them had any idea how to actually maintain not

only a healthy weight but a healthy attitude about our bodies

whatsoever.

Out of desperation, I became bulimic. And, because I am

an active researcher, I learned very quickly how to do it "the

right way" by eating a scoop of vanilla ice cream to help

things come up easier.   What a brilliant idea! I could eat

whatever I wanted, and then throw it all up! Of course, the

results weren't what I wanted them to be, and I could tell that

it was starting to take over my life. I finally broke down and told my parents that I was bulimic, and needed help with my health. "But you're not skinny enough to have an eating disorder. You're just doing this for attention," they said. Great. So I wasn't even doing an eating disorder the right way.

Upon doing my own research on how to heal my eating disorder myself since no one was chomping at the bit to help me, I discovered a website dedicated to something I had never heard of before:

Body Dysmorphic Disorder:

A psychological disorder in which a person becomes obsessed with imaginary defects in their appearance. Sometimes believing they are mutated, much heavier or smaller than appear in real life.

Hang Up Your Hang Ups

That definitely sounded like something I had been wrestling with this entire time. Not only was my weight the center of most conversations about me, but my looks in general were. I hyper focused on several points. I hated my uneven skin, my nose was too big, and my lack of torso made weight gain in my mid section the most uncomfortable burden I carried physically and mentally.

Around this time, MySpace was all the rage. If you wanted to speak to your friends from school, you had to have one. And if you had one, you had to have photos of yourself. I remember the very first time I ever had my photo taken not against my will. I was fourteen. I did my hair and makeup to the best of my ability. I put on my favorite t-shirt. I set the camera's self-timer to ten seconds and walked back across the room. I winced when it went off, as if in pain, and went to see

the mutant that would most certainly be staring back at me in the preview screen. Imagine my shock when the girl I saw in the photo wasn't a mutant at all. Sure, she was a bit chubby, but the lighting had evened out my skin, and my nose didn't look so big after all! Seeing myself in a viewfinder was the first time that I could actually accept who I was and what I looked like. After that, I began to stage elaborate (for a fourteen-year-old) photo shoots with outfits I made and had put together.

I learned how to hide the things I didn't want to show, and accentuate what photographed well. I figured out what fabrics were best for on and off camera, and how to copy the poses I saw in magazines. At school, I was the chubby, pimply girl with big hair who liked old music.

Hang Up Your Hang Ups

At home, I had this world that I created in which I was slam squad, stylist, model, and photographer all in one. When I was in my zone, I could accept myself in every way, shape, and form. When out in the "real world", my BDD could get the most of me. If someone didn't like me, it was because I wasn't pretty enough. If I was teased, it was because I wasn't good enough. If I wasn't accepted, it was my fault. It fed my social anxiety. Don't go out into the world. There are people out there who are waiting to tell you that you're not good enough. As time went on, and I posted more and more self-portraits, I was a size 14-16, but still practicing my styling skills, makeup artistry, and posing. I could create the girl in the photos. I liked her. Other people liked her too. And one day, I received an email asking me if I was available to be a plus size model...for money.

Imagine my shock. I leaped at the opportunity. My first experience on set was me feeling like an inconvenience because I was the biggest girl there. I powered through and did my job...and they kept calling me. To this day, the best way to explain to people how I feel is "I feel like the less attractive twin of the girl in the photos."

I kept on modeling as a plus size model for a few years. I never felt truly confident in myself during this time period. The other photographers didn't capture me in a way that I thought was flattering, and one even made me do a pin up photo shoot in which I'm eating a piece of pizza over and over again...as to point out something I didn't already know. I was a fat model. And fat is a fetish. I was depressed, and terribly unhealthy. I was carrying around an extra 50 pounds that were weighing me down in more ways than one. Anything

wrong with me, I would always blame on my size. If I didn't

get a job, it was because I was fat. If I got rejected, it's

because I wasn't thin enough. It was really easy to blanket all

of my problems with the simple excuse "It's just because I'm

fat."

And then, one day, something clicked. After spending yet

another day in bed, depressed, I ended up watching hours

upon hours of documentaries about diet and nutrition. I

decided to make the change from my junk food vegetarian

diet to a vegan lifestyle. The weight began to fall off of me.

Other people started to notice. My skin cleared up, my hair

and nails grew like crazy. My waist shrank to half its former

size. Imagine my shock when I realized that it didn't solve all

of my problems! It made them worse! I thought being thin

meant I would book more work. It didn't.

I thought skinny meant that I would be handed everything on a silver platter like my straight sized colleagues. Nothing happened. I thought that a skinny body would make the voices in my head stop telling me that I was disgusting. It didn't. They wouldn't stop unless I made them stop.

Over time, with counseling, healers, holistic doctors, and supportive friends, those voices have softened to a whisper when at one period of time, they were screams so loud, I could hear nothing else. But, as mentioned before, the BDD fuels social anxiety. My weight loss, in turn, made my clothes that used to make me feel safe fall off of me. For most, this is a great problem. And it is. But it also makes getting dressed nearly impossible when you are first starting your journey. I have tried to remedy this situation by stocking a fairly well-rounded wardrobe for myself, but at one point, getting

dressed to go out at any given point could result in me crying on the floor, surrounded by jeans that fell off of me. "I just want clothes that fit!" I used to yell. And one day it clicked. I learned how to navigate my way around these problems. I learned that having certain things in my closet helped me not only get dressed in the morning but helped me hold my head a little higher throughout the day as well.

As I started to express myself more and more through what I put on my body, my voice grew more confident, I started to really focus on my business, and I saw my spirit and my profits rise. I want to give this gift that I have fought long and hard for to every single woman that needs this. Pain is only painful if we don't use it to help others with it. I took every single thing that I learned and applied it to my styling business where I help people every single day learn to express

themselves and heal their insecurities through finding their

personal style and owning it. I want to be able to help you do

the same for yourself.

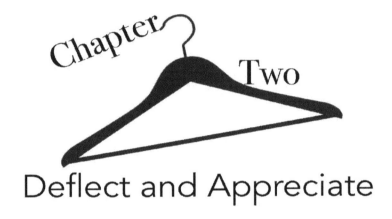

Chapter Two

Deflect and Appreciate

I am a stylist for a living. For those of you who don't know, a stylist is someone who handpicks the clothes and accessories for a multitude of projects such as film, print, ads, live performances, and public appearances. My career has been spent dressing people to look their best...usually very beautiful and famous people at that.

Payton Kemp Dale

One of my other jobs is as a model on runways and in photos. So, all of my income comes from either being paid to be photographed or making sure others look good in their photos and performances. Years of wanting to help others, and to be the person I needed for myself at sixteen, as well as an undying love for fashion have lead me to the career path of my dreams. I get to help people every single day! What more could a girl ask for? One of the main reasons why I wanted to even write this book in the first place was because of what has become inevitable in every single fitting I've ever done.

When I meet with my clients, the first thing I ask them is: What are you most comfortable with showing? This question could mean whatever they want it to mean. I have worked with several artists that didn't feel comfortable showing a lot of skin because their management wanted to brand them as

Hang Up Your Hang Ups

wholesome. But, when I get a client that has a laundry list of what they consider "problem areas" then I know that we have bigger fish to fry.

Everyone has their best features and their not so great features. That statement rings true from everyone. I've had supermodels, Grammy winners, CEOs of successful companies, and moms all tell me the exact same thing. "I hate my arms." or "My boobs aren't big enough." and the list goes on and on. Notice, that they never really answered my question. They took "What are you comfortable with showing?" and turned it into "What do you hate about yourself?"

I assure you that if you stand in front of the mirror naked long enough, you will find something to hate. I am so guilty of it.

Payton Kemp Dale

I did it this morning! My least favorite part about myself is my stomach. I have struggled with my weight as long as I can remember. My hips are covered in stretch marks.

The skin on my entire body is so sensitive, that the slightest thing breaks me out. So, when I was looking in the mirror today, and pulling faces at my uneven skin tone, and the food baby from last night that I was convinced the rest of the world could see, I have to talk myself down, just like I've talked many of the most beautiful people down. Here is an example of what one of those conversations look like.

Oh, god, oh god! I'm so fat right now. I can't stand to look at myself.

What makes you say that?

Hang Up Your Hang Ups

I just have this awful food baby from last night. My husband and I went out and got Indian food, and I knew I ate too much! I should have just-

Oh! Your husband took you out? That's so thoughtful! How was the food?

It was SOOOO good, girl! I ate WAY too much! But we had such a great time!

I hear ya! Indian is my favorite! I can understand that you may FEEL bloated, but you certainly don't look it. Let's get you into this outfit, and we can take a quick photo so you can see what I see.

Are you sure?

Absolutely. You are beautiful.

99.9 percent of the time this works. It isn't phony, it's the truth! Sometimes we fall down the rabbit hole of nitpicking ourselves to death. Find what triggers you. Is it stress that causes you to binge eat, and in return, hate your bloat? Is it scrolling through Instagram and looking at someone else who's perfectly toned, living their dream life? I am SO guilty of doing what's wrong.

But, I have managed to come up with a nice tool that I like to call DEFLECT AND APPRECIATE! Here's how it works.

What is something you don't like about yourself?

I don't like my stomach.

Why?

It is covered in stretch marks.

Hang Up Your Hang Ups

What made it that way?

I got stretch marks from losing weight.

Deflect-How could that be made into a good thing?

My body knew that the extra weight I was carrying was bad

for me.

Who would you be without this thought about

yourself?

I would probably be more focused on what's really

important in my life. I could focus that energy on helping

others if I wasn't so preoccupied with it.

Turn it around. Appreciate your flaw.

I have stretch marks from losing weight. By losing weight, it

was easier for me adapt to a healthier lifestyle, that will

benefit me in the long run. I am grateful for my stretch marks because they are a sign of how far I have come!

Do this with everything you cannot stand about yourselves. It may take you an hour, or it may take you days, but I want you to go through every single little thing that you feel makes you less than worthy.

Maybe you don't like your boobs because they lost their "oomph" after you had a few babies. You can be grateful that your body was strong enough to bring life in this world. Perhaps you aren't fond of your big feet. Your feet hold you up! And you've got them! Not everyone does! How lucky are you?

After you're done with your list, I want you to do something for me. Take a photo of what you don't like about

Hang Up Your Hang Ups

yourself. Document what you despise. I took nude photos

on my phone (deleted them afterward) and realized that even

though I may not like my skin, and I might focus too much on

my stomach that isn't "perfect", in the grand scheme of

Payton, it's really not all that noticeable! Snap as many photos

as it takes to learn to appreciate that part of your body. I then

want you to hang up your hang ups. Put them in the back of

the closet that is your mind. We only want the most beautiful

pieces to be front and center. Bad self-talk is like the ratty old

sweatpants you've had since college. They're a fact of life,

and you may hold on to them, but we don't need that to be

the first thing we see when it comes to selecting your

thoughts for the day.

So, it's your turn. Grab a pen, and fill these out.

1. What is something you don't like about yourself physically?

_____

_____

_____

_____

_____

_____

_____

Hang Up Your Hang Ups

2. Why?

_____

_____

_____

_____

_____

_____

_____

_____

3. What made it that way?

_____

_____

_____

_____

_____

_____

_____

_____

Hang Up Your Hang Ups

4. Deflect-How could that be made into a good thing?

_____

_____

_____

_____

_____

_____

_____

_____

5. Who would you be without that thought?

_____

_____

_____

_____

_____

_____

_____

_____

_____

Hang Up Your Hang Ups

6. Turn it around. I appreciate my _____ because _____.

_____

_____

_____

_____

_____

_____

_____

_____

Payton Kemp Dale

Learn to select your thoughts about yourself just as you would select what you are wearing for the day. And your limiting beliefs are just like that old pair of sweatpants you've had since college. They're tired, they're unflattering, and they aren't doing you any favors. Time to retire them.

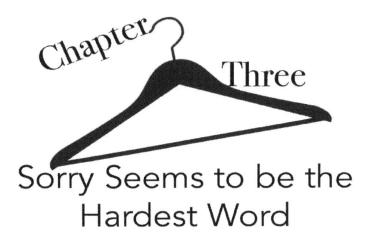

Chapter Three

Sorry Seems to be the Hardest Word

Did you do the homework from the last chapter? Good!

Now that we have identified our least favorite parts of

ourselves, let's move on from there. We are going to talk

about why we have those crazy notions floating around in our

heads. Because guess what? You came into this world

without any sort of care or consideration about how big your

thighs were. Do you seriously think that when you were learning how to walk that you were wrapped up in how chunky your arms were, and how they jiggled with each step? Of course not! So, when did we get so messed up? Without the risk of sounding completely like a Debbie Downer here, it's sort of an inevitability that by the time you reach a certain age, the world has already screwed you up in some way, shape, or form. But I have fantastic news for you. It's not your fault that you're screwed up! It's your fault if you stay screwed up.

Children as early as five years old are now concerned with getting fat. According to a recent study, little girls as young as seven have tried some sort of dieting behavior. The last I checked, the numbers for women in America who have eating disorders are around 20,000,000. I still think that number is

Hang Up Your Hang Ups

much too low, because most women never really think they

have an eating disorder, but suffer from disordered eating,

which if you are a woman over the age of eighteen reading

this book, I will bet my vintage Louis Vuitton bags that you

have at one point in your life.

So, the good news is, you're not alone! But, how do we

prevent this stuff from happening to the future generations of

badass leaders, mothers, and the first female president? How

can women help heal the world if we are too busy worrying

about the circumference of our bellies? Education, of course!

The first step in arming ourselves with knowledge is to

attack our own insecurities at the root. By learning where our

negative self-talk began, we have to do a little time traveling.

I'll use one of my own examples.

Payton Kemp Dale

1. What is your limiting belief?

I am too fat. I am gross. My stomach is too big.

2. Who told you these things?

My entire family said mean things about my weight. But, what really bothered me is when I watched my beautiful mom stand in front of the mirror and pick herself apart completely.

3. How did it make you feel?

That if she were "fat" and "gross" and she was smaller than me, that I must be enormous, and disgusting. It never even crossed my mind that my mother wasn't beautiful. So, if my beautiful mother weren't good enough, I must be a mutant. It made me depressed.

4. Where was that person at emotionally when those things were said?

Hurting. Feeling insecure and scared. She was a single mom going through chemo at the time, and I can't imagine how scary that must have been.

5. Was that person hurting?

Absolutely.

6. Could you show that person some compassion?

Now, as an adult, I can see where she was at emotionally. I can definitely empathize with her. I would tell her that she was so much more than her looks. I would tell her that she was brave, and to stop worrying about her looks, because she needed to fight. I don't tell her nearly enough how brave she was.

Do this with every single person that has ever made you feel bad about the way you look. Maybe you're not at a place where you feel comfortable reaching out to them physically. But, write it down. Write down all of the questions from above and answer them on paper. There is something magical about writing things down. It makes them true! This will be a huge step in healing your relationship with those that have hurt you. And now that we have forgiven those around us, it's time to arm ourselves with how to guard our hearts when it comes to the media!

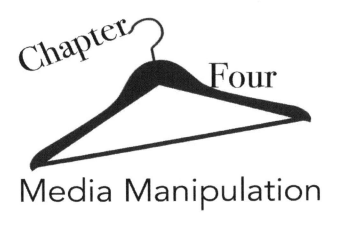

Media Manipulation

On average, women see an average of 5,000 ads a day. Compare this to the 500 advertisements that women saw forty years ago, and it's no wonder why we are more preoccupied with our looks more than ever! Just the other morning I woke up, took the dogs out, and made some coffee. In the time it took me to get my kettle to boil, I scrolled through my newsfeed and counted a total of 46

47

advertisements in the six minutes it took to make a french press. The ads were full of skinny, tanned, muscular, young women with mermaid hair and extra white smiles. Phrases like "SKINNY TEA" "WAIST TRAINERS" and "THREE CUP SIZES LARGER!" flashed before my eyes. The sponsored posts were cleverly tucked in between friends' posts of their kids, vacations, and lunch photos. It was almost like scrolling through my Instagram feed was like entering the ocean and being stung by insecurity jellyfish. Suddenly, I was bombarded with products to make my skin clearer, my waist smaller, and my hair flow like a damn Disney princess.

I consider myself to be a pretty smart cookie. But after I caught the sight of myself in the reflection of the toaster oven, I couldn't help but start to get a little down.

Hang Up Your Hang Ups

With my unkempt hair, a fresh breakout growing on my chin, and my glasses askew on my nose, I was a far cry from the Instagram models staring back at me from my phone. The jellyfish started to sting! ZAP! You need something for that skin of yours! ZAP! Is that a food baby from last night? I had to stop and remind myself something that I have known consciously for years. The fashion and beauty industry WANTS me to feel this way! Beauty and fashion is a trillion dollar industry that thrives on insecurities. Imagine if we didn't think that every single bump or flaw on our face didn't have a cream to "perfect" it! What would we buy then? We wouldn't buy anything! Of course, this is common knowledge! But if it's so common, then why are we still stressing over lumps and bumps? I'll tell you why! Marketing.

We are exposed to 10.4 hours of media a day. This is what is known as passive consumption. Scrolling through Instagram, seeing an ad before a video, and driving by billboards are just a few examples of passive consumption. Don't even get me started on how many hours gets added onto that number when you binge watch your favorite TV show. In that time, we are exposed to roughly 56 ads an hour. So, you do the math on that one. We see a lot of freaking ads, you guys. The advertising executives are sneakier these days about how they go about getting their message across. Take natural advertising for example.

Natural advertising, also known as native content is a clever way of disguising an ad by camouflaging it to match the platform on which it appears.

Hang Up Your Hang Ups

Take all of those online quizzes, for example. "What sort of wallpaper are you?" seems like a normal quiz to take. The questions look exactly the same as the "Which potato are you?" questions, but after you've completed the test, you are sent a link to a realtor's office. Aha! They've fooled you into thinking that you're decorating your imaginary house when really they are just trying to sell you on a neighborhood realtor. Genius! And they do it all of the time! Open any fashion magazine, and you will see campaigns for cosmetic companies that look just like the articles in the magazines! You'll notice phrases like "Sponsored Ad" or "Sponsored by" in tiny print somewhere. But, if you're just passively glancing over it the way many of us consume our media, then you will miss the fact that you are being sold something!

Payton Kemp Dale

BuzzFeed is notorious for natural advertising. There was a thread the other day that I saw for "Chubby Girl Struggles" that listed a ton of hilarious, yet relatable issues that overweight women deal with. After I got to the bottom of the article, there was a diet pill ad right there. They didn't even try to hide it!

The first time I really thought about how I was being marketed to was when I picked up the book "Healthy Is The New Skinny" by Katie Willcox. Katie is a plus size model who is open about her struggles with body image over the years. She also is the first person in the industry to my knowledge that really started to question what we were doing to women by not asking any questions about why we went about things this way.

Hang Up Your Hang Ups

Katie's book definitely shaped the way I shop, how I question things and even began to help me avoid those dressing room meltdowns!

In order to thrive, the beauty industry in this country has to be completely unattainable. If the beauty standard is something everyone can go out and get, and we wake up one morning deciding that everyone is beautiful, we won't purchase products. If I decided that my skin was fine, I'm not going to buy any more lotions and potions. My hair is fine the way it is, so I won't purchase any miracle conditioners for it. I think my waist is fine the way it is, so there goes hundreds and thousands of dollars spent on diet programs, pills, and waist trainers. There's at least a few hundred dollars of products I've decided I no longer need. Imagine if we all did that. The industry would go broke!

But they're not going to make it that easy to get away from. Nope! Crippling insecurity isn't like being an alcoholic who avoids the bar. Because now with the internet the way that it is, whatever you've searched for over the course of your lifetime is what determines the ads you see! A few years ago, I once spent a few minutes looking at "full acne coverage makeup" videos, and to this day I see pop-ups for zit creams, dermatologists, and $54 masks made of charcoal and gold flake. If you've ever looked for workout videos online, suddenly there are now sidebars full of diet pills, and deals on leggings and sports bras. It starts to creep into your brain, and the more you see it, the more you believe! There is no escaping advertising.

The language used in these campaigns can also be quite shady as well. A fantastic example that Katie cites in her book

Hang Up Your Hang Ups

is how an entire generation of women began smoking because of one ad. During the Suffragette Era of the 1900's, there was suddenly an idea to double the numbers of cigarette smokers in America. The women who were marching for the right to vote were the new targets for the tobacco industry. "TORCHES OF FREEDOM" was stamped on promotions for cigarettes everywhere. By telling women that they would be liberated if they just lit up, an entirely new demographic of women picked up a nasty habit. That idea of freedom that they bought so willingly was just a corporate plot. Talk about equality between the sexes! The same thing happened a few years ago when a Victoria's Secret Angel was interviewed telling the cameraman that her wings made her feel "empowered" as she sexily struts along in her push up bra that cost more than my entire house. These buzzwords are snuck in the same way a mom sneaks kale into smoothies

for her kids. You don't know that it's happening, but it goes down pretty easy!

So, knowing that there are lots of greedy people wanting to sell you things doesn't feel all that great, I'll admit. But we can now use this knowledge to arm ourselves before we go out into the world or even scarier...the dressing room! But, we will talk about the dressing room later on. You think I would let you go without homework? Don't you know me by now?

Hang Up Your Hang Ups

Answer these questions below.

1. What was the last piece of clothing or cosmetic that you bought?

_____

_____

_____

_____

_____

_____

_____

_____

2. Why did you buy it? Was it because you wanted to? Or

was it because you felt like you HAD to?

_____

_____

_____

_____

_____

_____

_____

_____

Hang Up Your Hang Ups

3. How did you find out about the product?   If it was an

ad, answer the question below.

_____

_____

_____

4. What did the ad promise you in return for buying this

product? What kind of language did they use?

_____

_____

_____

_____

5. How did you feel after your purchase?

_____

_____

_____

_____

_____

_____

_____

_____

Hang Up Your Hang Ups

Of course, I love my makeup and my clothes. I could spend hours getting ready if given the chance. But, now before I buy anything, I ask myself these few questions. Am I buying this for myself because I want to? Or, am I buying this for myself because I feel inadequate in some way, and this promised to make me feel better? Think about how you are being targeted as a female consumer when you go shopping, and remember what I said:

The beauty standard in this country must be unattainable in order to sell you products.

Repeat this to yourself over and over again until it clicks. Rinse, lather, repeat. You got this! Now, let's move on to the FUN part of this journey! Let's find your personal style!!!

Chapter Five

Find Your Own
Personal Style

Now that we've tackled most of the emotional side of fully

owning our most fabulous selves, I want to talk to you guys

about style. Most people seem to think that fashion is a

frivolous industry built on the insecurities of women. While as

we discussed in the previous chapter that some of that is true,

Hang Up Your Hang Ups

we can also use expressing ourselves through the way that we dress as a healing tool!

What would you say your personal style is right now?

A fashion blog I once worked with called my style "Rockstar Wife Chic" which was a joke at the time but slowly became my signature look.

Did it look like a member of The Rolling Stones or one of their wives wore it?

If so, then it's probably in my closet!

Immediately I am transported to a different time and place when that phrase is uttered. Paisley, velvet, leopard, silks, tribal jewelry, hats and being just a little *too much* in general spring to mind when I hear "Rockstar Wife Chic" and while my style has evolved ever so slightly over the years, the

overall feeling has remained the same. When people see me and then hear that I'm married to a guitar player, they nod their heads and say, "Of course you are."

There are several million different styles out there. Do you find yourself to be a preppy classic, tomboy, bohemian, urban, all American, minimalist, or stylistically challenged? Most of my clients respond with "frumpy mom" or "leggings all day." When I ask these women if they are happy with what their clothing says about them right now, nine times out of ten the answer is a big fat NO. Sure, finding your own personal style sounds easy enough until you actually step foot into a mall! Have you been in one lately? They're awful! The minute you step through the doors you are greeted by screaming children, an overwhelming scent of burnt Cinnabon's, and hundreds upon hundreds of different ads

telling you what you need to buy right this very minute! But if you have a game plan and know who you are at your core, it actually can be pretty fun. Here's how to figure out your own personal style.

The first thing I like to ask my clients at this stage is who their celebrity style crushes are. This helps me to identify the similarities that each of those women has so we can find out the common ground. The common denominator of all of your style icons is truly the root of what your own personal style is. So let's use me as an example. When I was fifteen I saw a photo of all of The Beatles' wives. The photo was this gorgeous psychedelic campaign for a boutique that sold hippie clothes. The women wore bright colors, lots of jewelry, and all had the same haircut. Jane Birkin, Bianca Jagger, and Brigitte Bardot were style icons I later discovered. I took what

all of these women had in common, and found my middle

ground.   My signature look of bangs, bell bottoms, big

sunglasses and even bigger shoes came from taking bits of all

of those women and interpreting them in my own way.

Next, I ask my clients if what they are currently wearing on

a regular basis reflects how they feel on the outside.   Many

times the woman who wears nothing but drab sweatpants

doesn't want to be looked at.   Maybe she's put on weight, or

maybe she's going through a bad breakup, but those

shapeless sweats are her everyday look.   Often when I see a

stylistically challenged woman, the outside reflects how she

feels about herself inside.   These days I usually feel like a

badass woman that is married to a super hot guitar player.

My outfits tend to reflect that.   It wasn't always this way.

When I was insecure and felt like my body was something to

Hang Up Your Hang Ups

hate, I covered it in yards and yards of fabric. I wore jeans in the summertime when it was 100 degrees outside. My hair was always scraped up on my head in a greasy topknot because I wasn't special enough to be looked at. What did it matter if I didn't wash my hair anyway?

The point was made loud and clear that I was unworthy of being looked at. So I did everything in my power to remain invisible. I see so many women do this on a regular basis. But I've got bad news for you, girlfriend. We can all see you.

Do you dress the way you do currently because you feel like it's an accurate representation of who you are? Or do you dress this way because you are stuck in a rut? Ask yourself this every time you look in the mirror. I know that so many women after they give birth decide that now that they're a

mom that they don't need to take care of themselves. This often results in the sweatpants as everyday wear, neglecting your self-care, and ignoring your own needs while dealing with everyone else's. It's like the saying that you can't pour from an empty cup. You can not take care of others unless you take care of yourself first! This is self-care. It is a priority, not an option.

Hang Up Your Hang Ups

I want you to ask yourself a few questions about your outfit before you leave the house.

1. Does this outfit currently fit my lifestyle? Can I accomplish everything I need to do today in this look?

_____

_____

_____

_____

_____

_____

_____

2. Does this fit who I am as a person now? A lot of women get stuck in their club wear days, wearing bandage dresses from the mall a little past their expiration date.

_____

_____

_____

_____

_____

_____

_____

3. Am I furthering negative self-talk when I wear this? Are you wearing the potato sack to hide the "pooch" your mom told you to suck in? Are your arms covered because you feel like women over a certain age shouldn't show their arms?

_____

_____

_____

_____

_____

_____

4. Are you dressing this way because you WANT to, or because you feel like you have to? Did you put this outfit on today because it makes you extremely happy? Or are you wearing it because you feel like it's what you SHOULD be wearing?

Hang Up Your Hang Ups

This is how we get stuck in style ruts. I know that in the middle of my weight loss journey I got stuck in a rut of my very own. When I was in between sizes, I lived in mumus and caftans. My collection of mumus would rival Mrs. Roper's. I held on to these pieces for so long, until one day my husband pointed out to me that every time I eat a big meal, I gravitate towards the oversized tents. Any time I mentioned not feeling like I was up to par with my fitness, he noticed I grabbed one of my security blankets. Even I didn't realize this pattern, and I dress people for a living! So, while the mumus fit into my rockstar wife look, it was becoming something I was relying too heavily upon. They went to the back of my closet where they will live to see another day. But the difference is now, they're no longer my safe place to hide.

After that moment I realized just how easy it was for women to fall into ruts without someone there to call them out on their own mess.

So, how do you figure out what your style is? How can you dodge putting yourself into a style funk? Before this all becomes too much to handle, here is my fashion formula for getting your game together no matter what size, age, or profession you are currently.

Pinterest is my best friend these days. Use it as a tool to help navigate all of the millions of photos of other people's outfits that you see on a regular basis. Figure out your style crushes. For instance, a client of mine really loved Sarah Jessica Parker's style. She sent me some photos of outfits SJP had worn lately. One was a tulle skirt with a beautiful corset top, the other was boyfriend jeans with a blazer. In true Sarah

Hang Up Your Hang Ups

Jessica Parker form, she was accessorized perfectly and looked chic in everything. My client wanted help translating this into her everyday life.

I pointed out the details in the outfit photos to my client. What held these two looks together was that they were both eclectic and feminine. The tiny bows on the ballet flats were a subtle nod to a girly girl, while a blazer and statement necklace paired nicely with an otherwise straight-laced piece of menswear. Aside from noticing little style staples that keep our style crushes outfits all looking put together and on brand, my client also failed to realize something else. Sarah Jessica Parker's body type was entirely different than her own. This is the moment where most women give up, decide that fashionable clothes aren't meant for them, and doom themselves to an eternity in leggings. But fear not!

Remember when I said to make a list of all of your icons and see what they had in common? As I pointed out to my client, the underlying themes were in every last one of SJP's looks! So, I had her type in "Eclectic Curvy Style" into her search tab.

She was bombarded with hundreds of fashion bloggers who have already done the hard work and translated that style into one more suitable for her body type!

This can be done with any icon and body type you may have. Another client of mine recently was distraught that she would never look like her fashion icon, Kate Moss. My client stood a few inches taller, and definitely a few sizes larger than the supermodel. Instead of trying to find another influence that shared her body type, she was on the verge of giving up. I asked for the images of Kate that inspired her so much.

Hang Up Your Hang Ups

When I opened them I immediately saw that all of the pieces were not only available in her size, but would be so flattering! I recalled a recent editorial of one of my favorite curvy models wearing an outfit nearly identical to one of Kate's.

Twenty minutes later, my client had ordered her first vegan leather jacket, bell bottom jeans, and platform heels to wear with her vintage rocker tees. Much better than sweatpants!

We can also look to our personal style heroes for beauty inspiration as well! I cut bangs into my hair when I realized that every single woman I thought was beautiful had this haircut! If you really admire someone's hair or makeup, I assure you that there is a video out there walking you through how to do it as well! Style is head to toe! Have fun with it. Don't be afraid to try new things. None of these decisions have to be permanent.

If you are feeling a little self-conscious right about now because of how your body currently looks, it's going to show through no matter how cute your outfit may be. I will bet money that there are pieces of clothing out in this great big universe that will fit not only your body but will enhance your beauty on the inside. Style gives you permission to be yourself! So, whenever you get wrapped up into thinking that you're not the same size as the women you admire, just remember! There is a reason why what you see is resonating with you. If you're looking at Kate Moss looking like a total badass in her leather pants and leopard boots and you feel a pang of sadness because you don't look like that, you're really just suppressing your inner badass spirit! It's just dying to get out! You're borrowing her vibe, not making a copy! And also...

COOL ISN'T A SIZE. IT'S AN ATTITUDE.

When your outside matches how incredible you feel on the inside, your entire life is going to change. Once you feel like a walking representation of yourself not only will you hold your head up higher, but you'll show up more for your business, your partner, your kids, whatever it is. The extra pep in your step is going to make a world of a difference. When you walk out of the house wearing your mom jeans or your baggy sweats, don't forget that WE CAN STILL SEE YOU. You actually draw more attention to yourself when you don't try. Take this example.

There are two moms on the playground at your kids' school. There is one mom who is wearing her husband's stained sweatshirt, shower shoes and oversized basketball shorts. Next to her stands a mom in a pair of jeans that fit, a t-shirt, and a cute motorcycle jacket with some ballet flats.

Hang Up Your Hang Ups

Let's add on a scarf for some extra flair. Both took equal time

in the morning to get dressed. Which person do you think is

going to stand out more to you?   Which one will you pay

more attention to? The mom that had her outfit plan down is

going to be someone that you might pause and think "Oh,

she's a cute mom." and go about your day. The other mom is

going to stand out like a sore thumb.   It might sound crazy,

but when you leave the house looking like you didn't try, you

actually will not only not be invisible, you will stand out more.

How you decide to dress will not only dictate how worthy you

feel, but how others will look at you.   This includes your

children. I know that moms are superheroes in real life. I

don't expect you all to get a blowout every week, wear fake

eyelashes, or contour yourself into oblivion. But Jesus Christ!

Put on real pants!

Payton Kemp Dale

Show your kids that they are worthy of owning real pants! When you walk out into the world with your chin up, representing a confident woman who feels good enough, they will see that.

Your self-care today will affect generations of women for years to come. Please don't set the example that women can't be put together AND smart. We have come way too far to feel that way. We can see you, moms! And your kids are watching too! Let's show them how important it is to take care of ourselves.

Hang Up Your Hang Ups

So now it's time for your homework!

1. Make a list of your style icons.

*　_____

*　_____

*　_____

*　_____

*　_____

*　_____

*　_____

*　_____

*　_____

Payton Kemp Dale

2. What do they all have in common?

_____

_____

_____

_____

_____

_____

_____

_____

Hang Up Your Hang Ups

3. What pieces would you like to see hanging in your personal closet?

_____

_____

_____

_____

_____

_____

_____

_____

4. And now you get to make a Pinterest (or regular college if that's your bag) of what your new personal style is all about. Add outfits, color schemes, quotes...whatever tickles your fancy. You're going to be using this when you go shopping!

_____

_____

_____

_____

_____

_____

_____

Hang Up Your Hang Ups

5. And the last one...how do you want to feel when getting dressed in the morning?

_____

_____

_____

_____

_____

_____

_____

In the next chapter, we are going to be discussing getting your closet cleaned out to make room for your beautiful new clothes. It's hard to feel like the badass warrior princess that you are when you are in danger of being swallowed up by an avalanche of clothes that no longer fit!

Chapter Six

Cleaning Out Your Closet

Before we go out and shop for our new clothes we have to

do the not so fun part. We have to clean out your closet!

Give all the new and beautiful clothes and accessories you're

about to bring into your home the space to breathe! This

chapter might seem like this is going to be a daunting task,

but I promise you that you'll feel so much better when you're done! You may actually have fun!

Invite one of your friends over. If your friends don't live close by you can always FaceTime them! Bribe them with fancy lattes, or a bottle of wine to sip on while they help you tackle this project. Having the moral support there will not only be beneficial to get it done, but it will also help to have a critical eye to tell you whether or not you need to ditch certain things hanging in your closet. Find a good playlist on Spotify to listen to while you're going to town on the pile of clothes. Make it like a bad movie montage. Once you have the BFF in place, the perfect soundtrack, and a great caffeine buzz going, it's time to get to work.

First thing's first. I want you to take every single thing that is in your closet and throw it on your bed. No, really. If

Hang Up Your Hang Ups

everything is on your bed, you will absolutely HAVE to tackle it today. No excuses! After you've removed every last item in your wardrobe, I want you to make the following piles:

KEEP: Pieces that currently fit, that make you feel good, and/or are staple pieces. We will get to what a staple piece is in the next chapter.

SELL: Clothes that don't fit, don't make you feel good, or no longer serve you, but are in great shape. I personally love selling stuff like this on apps like Poshmark. You can then use that money to shop for your new stuff!

DONATE: Stuff that maybe isn't quite worth much to sell, but someone will benefit from it goes in this pile. Bonus points on this one because most charities will give you a slip for your tax write offs!

TOSS: Self-explanatory. We don't need your stained granny panties in here.

Let's talk about a few things that definitely do **NOT** belong in your KEEP pile.

YOUR "GOAL" JEANS: Or little black dress, or bikini. Whatever you purchased in a smaller size to one day fit into. These pieces actually make you feel worse about yourself and will be a constant reminder of you not loving your body right now as it is. And we aren't about that life. Sell it to buy something that you love right now, or give it away to someone who could use it.

THINGS THAT SPARK BAD MEMORIES FOR YOU: Maybe it's the dress you wore on your first date with your ex or a wedding dress from a failed marriage.

Hang Up Your Hang Ups

Perhaps it's a dress you wore when you were smaller, and it reminds you that you're not as small as you want to be anymore. It could be a t-shirt you wore the day your dog got put to sleep (I threw mine out, even though I loved that shirt) But if it reminds you of something that makes you sad, get rid of it!

GIFTS YOU FEEL GUILTY FOR NOT LIKING: Whether it's the ugly Christmas sweater your grandma bought you or a pair of earrings a distant relative sent you for graduation...if you haven't worn it, hate it, and it's taking up valuable real estate in your closet, chuck it!

CLOTHES YOU HAVEN'T WORN IN THE LAST YEAR: If you really love something, you'll wear it. If you don't remember the last time you wore it, get rid of it.

After your piles have been made, load up your donation pieces and get them out of your space. That extra clutter will only result in a headache. Take what you are selling to the nearest consignment shop.

If you are selling online, keep those items in a separate suitcase, or in a box in a space that's not your closet. You need to have all of the empty closet space open so we can visualize what needs to go in it. Next thing I highly recommend is to get yourself matching hangers. Merchandising your closet is an absolute must if you really want to keep that space neat and organized. I love the black space saving velvet hangers. You can buy these cheaply in bulk. Opening your closet every day to see a clean, organized space full of pieces you absolutely love will make you start your day on the right foot.

NOW, IT'S TIME TO SHOP!

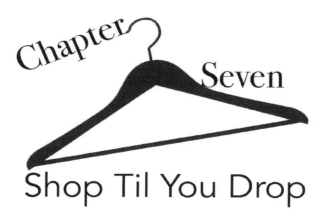

Chapter Seven

Shop Til You Drop

Congratulations! You've conquered the hard part! Surely

going shopping isn't as big of a deal as tackling your body

image concerns head on! Right? Well, not quite. In this

chapter, we are going to talk about not only what should be in

your finished closet, but also how to avoid dressing room

meltdowns, and how to get the most bang for your buck! But

first, I'm going to throw some math at you.

Hang Up Your Hang Ups

I know what you're thinking! "MATH!? In a style book?! Why?!" But, this formula will help you when deciding if what you're looking at will be a wise investment.

THE COST PER WEAR FORMULA

(Cost of item) divided by (Times I can wear this piece)

The cost per wear formula is fantastic for those moments where you can't decide if something is actually worth buying! For instance, say I need a black blazer. The options I have in this scenario are to go to the local fast fashion store at my mall and spend $19.99 on one or go to a higher end department store and spend $60 for one that's on sale. You may think that $19.99 is a better move to make financially, but here's something else to take into consideration.

Generally speaking, you get what you pay for when it comes to clothes.

So, let's say you buy that $19.99 blazer. You wear it twice and wash it. It completely falls apart. So before tax, you've spent a little under $10.00 per wear before having to replace it again. Take the $60 blazer now. You buy that jacket and take great care of it. You wear it once a week for four years. Congratulations, smart shopper. You paid around $3.50 per wear for it. Quality over quantity always!

When shopping, it's important to first look for staple pieces. Staple pieces are the basics that will hold your wardrobe together. The following list is what I personally think everyone should have in their closets.

Hang Up Your Hang Ups

1. White t-shirt

2. Grey or black t-shirt or tank

3. Long or ¾ length sleeve basic tee in white, striped, or black

4. Button down shirt

5. Little Black Dress (aka the "LBD)

6. Blazer (in black, navy or gray)

7. A pair of jeans that FIT. Get these tailored if you have to.

8. Ankle boots

9. Nude and black heels

10. Your version of a flat shoe

This list may seem rather boring, but you can't expect for the many elements of your outfit to be held together without staples. All of the pieces listed above can easily be styled to fit into whatever category you fall under. So, let's take my fun and flirty client that loves Sarah Jessica Parker. She paired a plain white tee with a poofy tulle skirt, heels, and statement jewelry. Another one of my clients really gravitated towards minimalist chic. Her white tee was paired with boyfriend jeans and a classic pair of Converse. Your version of a little black dress may be something sleek and sophisticated, while mine is a flowing more bohemian look with bell sleeves and embroidered detail. I frequently wear blazers with vintage band shirts. You might wear yours with a sensible sweater and pearls. The point here is that every single woman needs these pieces to keep her style held together.

Hang Up Your Hang Ups

If not, you have a closet full of kimonos and nothing to wear them with! But, seriously you guys, that was my problem a few years ago...

Now that your closet is stashed with a plethora of pieces to help keep it together, let's shop for the fun stuff!

It's time for the wow pieces! Wow pieces are extra items in your closet that make you feel incredible. These are going to be the pieces where you can really let your personality shine through. It's good to have a game plan before we go shopping, though. So here are a few tips I like to use when I go looking for my clients.

Have a shopping game plan. Make a budget and stick to it. Maybe your budget is $200 for one season. Maybe it's $20,000.

Whatever you are planning to spend, make sure that's all you spend. Keep that Pinterest board saved on your phone and make a list of what you're hoping to leave the store with.

Setting an intention for what you hope to accomplish for the day will set you up for success even if you leave empty-handed.

Use your style crushes as muses for your shopping. Ask yourself "Would (insert fashion icon here) wear this?" If not, you can move on. This helps take your own insecurities out of the mix. When your attention is focused on someone else it's a lot easier to not play into those insecurities that tend to creep in. You can pick and choose who you want to channel every time you shop or get dressed in the morning! That's the great thing about having influences.

Hang Up Your Hang Ups

You can have more than one!

Look for clothing that mimics your body shape. This is a great little hack for when you're trying to decide if something is worth bringing back to the dressing room. If you're straight up and down like Twiggy, then go for that column dress!

If you're rocking an hourglass figure, then look at how that wrap dress hangs on that hanger! If it looks that good on the hanger, imagine what it'll look like on you! If you are curvier, it may seem counterintuitive to look for clothes that aren't tents, but hear me out! If you wear clothes that flatter and fit your body, you will look like the most babely version of yourself. Now I lean more towards the rectangular side of body types, so shapeless rectangles actually work on my body type.

However, when I was larger and had a fairly large chest, I favored babydoll dresses that cut off right at my boobs and fanned out right at my stomach. No wonder people thought I was pregnant. That giant bunch of fabric accentuated the belly I had underneath my already uncomfortably large breasts! Duh! After I learned to look for garments that mimicked my body shape on the hanger, I started to gravitate towards more tailored pieces.

Without going to the gym I slimmed my frame instantly by changing my outfit!

The hanger trick works most of the time, but if you have the time, don't be afraid to try on different silhouettes to see what you like best. This is supposed to be fun!

Hang Up Your Hang Ups

Tags are a guideline not a definite. In women's fashion, tags are used for more of a guideline rather than an actual measurement. It's so fair, isn't it? We get to bleed for seven days and not die and we can never figure out what size we truly are. When you shop, don't think of tags as the end all. I have jeans that are a size 2 and jeans that are a size 8. They both fit the exact same. And I guarantee you that number doesn't measure how good you are at your job, or how great your homemade chocolate chip cookies are, or how great of a mom or wife or whatever you are. That number doesn't mean a thing, girlfriend.

Take time to try all of your fabulous new possible pieces on. But before you head to the dressing room, I wanted to give you some information on how to avoid that dreaded dressing room meltdown that we have all have.

Knowledge is power. Remember what we talked about in the chapter about media manipulation. The average model's body represents about 2% of the population. So we are bombarded with millions of images of women that we probably don't look like. If you saw the top you're trying on in a magazine before going to the store to try it on, remember this. That model had a glam squad. She had a stylist that steamed, pinned, taped, clipped, and maybe even sewed her into the top before she was photographed in it. There was a lighting crew that day to light every single inch of her body to make sure that everything popped just right. There was a makeup artist to make sure that her already flawless face looked even more perfect than it already is. Hair extensions were probably added in to give her the illusion of having a flowing mane.

Hang Up Your Hang Ups

The photographer took hundreds of photos from angles that we will never be able to accomplish with our front facing camera feature on our phones. And then a professional editor used Photoshop to make her look like an Amazonian goddess. I've been on glam squads like these. I've been the girl in these photos. The girls in the photos don't even look like the model in these campaigns! This is a great thing to remind yourself when you are starting to get down on yourself and start comparing your body to the one you saw in the magazine.

Different stores use different tricks in their dressing rooms to encourage you to buy things. There's a fast fashion chain which will remain nameless that springs to my mind. Fast fashion stores usually have dark dressing rooms with loud, overpowering music blasting over loudspeakers. They play

club music to increase a sense of urgency in you, and the rooms are kept dark so you don't see the poor quality of the clothing they are selling you. Once you get home and see what you bought, you're often left with a sense of regret for purchasing such poorly made clothes. There's a reason why they have a strict no return policy. On the other hand, most higher end retail stores use incredible lighting and some even go so far as to slant their mirrors slightly so you look longer and leaner. When you get home and try on those clothes, you wonder why you don't look as good in them at home as you did in the store! Keep in mind the environments you are shopping in and the tools they are using to sell you products. I like to bring a friend along to shop with me to take photos and videos so I can get a second opinion and see what the garments actually look like.

Hang Up Your Hang Ups

If you want to avoid all of the dressing room drama all together you can always shop online! Online shopping is a great alternative if you have some extra time and want to avoid the hustle and bustle of the mall or your local boutique. Everything gets shipped to your front door and you can try things on in the comfort of your own home. This is when it's really important to know your measurements so you can buy the appropriate sizes from different retailers. Just remember that the number on the tape measure doesn't measure how fabulous you are!

Rome wasn't built in a day, and your dream wardrobe won't be either. Don't get caught up in trying to have everything all at once. Don't feel pressured into buying every single thing in one place at one time. Space it out. Cultivating your personal style is like any other relationship. But once you have

it down to an art, you'll be glad you took the time to learn how to shop properly.

Once you get your fabulous new clothes and accessories home you can now put them away in your closet!

Aren't you glad you cleaned it out now? The space you have to work with will determine your organization system. I suggest all of my clients merchandise their closets in the same way they would a boutique.

When you walk into beautiful store, you are greeted with wonderful smells, usually some fabulous decor, and everything is neatly organized on matching hangers. Make it easy to shop your closet every morning. This needs to be an exciting part of your process, not something you dread.

Hang Up Your Hang Ups

Figure out how you want to feel when you get ready in the morning! Do you want to feel polished and professional? Maybe you want to feel sophisticated and chic. I personally like to feel glamorous with a bit of a rock n roll edge. Set the tone for your day when you get dressed!

I like to burn incense, listen to music, and sit at my makeup table that is in the corner of my closet. I look up at my vision board full of motivational quotes and goals I have to get myself pumped up for my day. My entire house is decorated in the same sort of bohemian way that definitely makes it easy to get into that zone of vintage glamor that I love. If you're feminine and soft, decorate the area around your dressing space with beautiful candles.

Buy yourself some flowers from the supermarket. Light a candle and play your favorite music. Even if you have only five minutes to get dressed, make it an event. No matter how small your space is, make it your sanctuary.

This ritual determines how you will feel for the rest of the day. You deserve to enjoy getting dressed in the morning.

Chapter Eight

Hello, Gorgeous!

There is a scene in the movie "Funny Girl" where Fanny

Brice (played by the fabulous Barbra Streisand) catches a

glimpse of herself in the full-length mirror of her apartment.

She adjusts the collar on her leopard skin coat, looks herself

113

up and down and says very matter of factly "Hello, gorgeous!" before walking away.

In the movie, it's a running theme that people have always called Fanny the ugly but funny girl.
In that moment she realizes that she truly is gorgeous and she OWNS IT. I hope that after reading this book you will have moments like that on a regular basis.

We live in a world that is pretty dead set on having women not realizing their full potential. Can you imagine the stuff we could accomplish if we weren't hyper-focused on the rolls we have when we sit down? Think of all of the good we could do in our communities by lifting each other up today...not twenty pounds from now. Doesn't it seem silly to be worried about the number of the tags of our jeans now that we know how things are marketed towards us?

Hang Up Your Hang Ups

So maybe we aren't the first generation of women who have been told that we aren't good enough. We definitely won't be the last. Whether it's the women of the 1920's binding their breasts to achieve the ideal flapper body or the women of today injecting fat into their lips, butts, and god knows what else, there will always be someone there to tell us we need to change. It is so rebellious to show up loving every single inch of yourself and wearing whatever the hell makes you feel your very best. I want you to throw all standards given aside and give a big middle finger to the corporations trying to prey on our insecurities. You guys know how much I love to be a rebel.

Obviously curing ourselves of all negative beliefs is not going to be an easy task. It will be a struggle every single day. But when you have finally learned to accept and love

yourself as you are today and dress in a way that lets your beautiful personality shine through, you will feel better. When you feel better, you send all of that delicious positive energy out into the world. Dress the body you have today in clothes you love. You're doing the world a service by showing up and being the most incredible version of you. You are here for a reason. Please don't let the fact that you think your smile is crooked or your skin is too pale or your arms are too jiggly ever let you forget that. The next generation of young women are looking to you to set an example. Your daughters are watching you to see how you talk about yourself, and how you present yourself to the world. Your language will become theirs. How would you like to hear them speak about themselves?

Hang Up Your Hang Ups

Are you going to show them a confident woman who knows exactly who she is and what she has to bring to the table? Or are you going to show her an insecure mess who feels like she's not good enough? They're watching.

The world needs you to show up and answer your calling. The phone is ringing. Don't send it to voicemail. When you finally get to pick up that call, do me a favor. Greet your calling with a big "HELLO, GORGEOUS!" and then you take what you've learned here and spread the word. Let's have little girls grow up thinking they can be president, or a boss, or the best mom in the world instead of becoming yet another woman that hates themselves and thinks their stomach is too jiggly to matter. Rebel. Love the absolute shit out of yourself and dress your body accordingly like your life depends on it. Because it does.

Made in the USA
Columbia, SC
22 November 2019